Estonia Travel Guide 2023

Exploring Estonia's Natural Wonders:Off-the-Beaten-Path Adventures for the Discerning Traveler", comprehensive guide on Top Attractions, food and Travel Essentials

Anabel C. Gerald

D1299875

Table of content

Estonia Introduction

Estonia is a small, pretty country in the north of Europe. It is bordered on the east by Latvia and the south by Russia. From pagan times to its current state as a technological society, the nation has a long and varied history.

Islands, lakes, bogs, and forests dominate Estonia's landscape. The country's regular excellence fills in as a draw for guests keen on open air exercises like climbing, setting up camp, and skiing.

Tallinn, the largest and capital of Estonia, is one of the most popular tourist destinations. One of Europe's best-preserved medieval towns, Tallinn's Old Town is a UNESCO World Heritage Site with Gothic-style architecture, cobblestone streets, and picturesque squares. Tallinn is home to the impressive Kadriorg Palace and park, the Kumu Art Museum, and the singular Seaplane Harbor Museum, in addition to the Old Town.

Another great place for tourists to visit is Tartu, the second-largest city in Estonia. Tartu is well-known for its university, which was established in 1632, as well as its stunning Old Town, which exudes a relaxed and energetic atmosphere. The AHHAA Science Center and the Estonian National Museum are two of the city's unique museums.

In addition, Estonia is home to numerous other cultural attractions, including contemporary art exhibitions and traditional folk festivals. The custom of "singing revolutions," in which thousands of Estonians gather to sing patriotic songs as a sign of national pride and unity, is one distinctive feature of Estonian culture.

Last but not least, Estonia is renowned for its achievements in the technology sector and innovative spirit. One of the most digitally advanced nations in the world, the nation is home to numerous startups, including Skype. Estonian society is distinguished by its technological and forward-thinking mentality, which makes it appealing.

In general, Estonia is an enchanting, meagerly populated country with much to offer guests concerning society, nature, and development.

Estonia Geography And Climate

Estonia is a small nation in northern Europe that is bounded by Latvia, Russia, and the Gulf of Finland. One of the smallest countries in Europe, the nation covers 45,226 square kilometers. The vast, low-lying coastal plain, extensive forests, numerous lakes, and numerous islands make up most of Estonia's geography.

The coastline of Estonia is jagged in the north, with numerous inlets, bays, and peninsulas. The western coast includes a long, slender series of promontories, some of which loosen up into the ocean to shape islands like Hiiumaa and Saaremaa. Suur Munamägi, the nation's highest peak, is only 318 meters high and can be found in the southeast of the country.

The climate of Estonia is influenced by the Baltic Sea, which is to the north and west of the country. The temperature is moderate, with relatively high humidity, mild summers, and cold winters. The average temperature in January, one of Estonia's coldest months, is between −6 and −14 degrees Celsius, while the average temperature in July, one of Estonia's warmest months, is between +15 and +20 degrees Celsius.

The country experiences average annual precipitation of 500 to 900 millimeters, with the west experiencing the most and the east experiencing the least. Estonia's weather conditions are likewise described by continuous changes, and the environment can shift significantly inside a solitary day because of the country's area in the Baltic locale.

The diverse climate and geography of Estonia, despite its small size, provide visitors with a variety of outdoor activities to enjoy. Estonia's natural beauty is a big part of why tourists come to the country to see the rugged coastline and islands, hike, and camp in the forests.

Estonia history

The history of Estonia, which dates back to the Bronze Age and goes back more than 4,000 years, is rich and complicated. The Finno-Ugric, Balt, and Viking peoples were among the various tribes and ethnic groups that once inhabited the area that is now Estonia.

In the thirteenth 100 years, after a significant stretch of Germanic and Scandinavian rule, Estonia was vanquished by the Teutonic Knights, and turned out to be important for the Livonian Confederation. After that, in the 16th century, Estonia was ruled by Sweden until it was given to Russia at the beginning of the 18th century due to the Great Northern War.

Estonia declared independence in 1918, following the fall of the Russian Empire in World War I. However, the country was occupied by Soviet forces in 1940 during World War II, ending Estonia's first period of independence after only 22 years. Estonia joined the Soviet Union after the war and remained a Soviet republic for fifty years.

In the late 1980s, Estonia's citizens organized rallies, strikes, and other activities to demand greater freedom from Soviet control. As a result, the country became a focal point of independence movements throughout the Soviet Union. After a failed coup attempt in Moscow in 1991, Estonia regained its independence and transformed into a democratic republic with a parliamentary system.

Estonia has become one of the world's most technologically innovative and advanced nations due to its significant economic growth and development since independence. Being the first nation to offer electronic voting and the birthplace of Skype are two notable achievements.

Getting to Estonia

1. By Air: Flying into Tallinn Airport, which is just 4 km from the city center, is the quickest way to reach Estonia. Tallinn Air terminal is served by numerous carriers, including Estonian Air, Ryanair, Lufthansa, Finnair, and SAS.

2. By Sea: From Helsinki, Stockholm, or St. Petersburg, you can take a ferry to Estonia for a scenic and leisurely journey. Tallinn has customary ship associations with these urban areas.

3. By Air: You can likewise effectively arrive at Estonia via land, either by transport or via vehicle. All of the neighboring nations, including Latvia, Lithuania, Russia, and Finland, can be reached by international bus. From other European nations, you can also drive into Estonia at a number of car border crossings.

4. Public Transport: When you show up in Estonia, you can utilize the country's solid public transportation framework to get around. Tallinn has an advanced arrangement of transports, cable cars, and streetcars, and there are likewise territorial transports and trains that interface the various pieces of the country.

Whichever technique you pick, I'm certain you'll live it up visiting Estonia. The nation has a rich culture and interesting history, as well as gorgeous regular landscape, so there is a lot to see and do!

Chapter 1: planning your trip

Best Time To Visit

The best chance to visit Estonia relies upon your inclinations and what you need to encounter during your outing. A comprehensive guide to the best time to visit Estonia is provided here.

Summer (June to August):

The best time to visit Estonia is during the summer, from June to August. The days are long and warm, with up to 18 hours of daylight per day. Outdoor activities like swimming, hiking, and exploring the country's stunning beaches are at their best during this time. The Tallinn Old Town Days, Viljandi Folk Music Festival, and Pärnu Weekend Festival are just a few of the many festivals and events that take place during the summer.

September through November:

Fall in Estonia can be a wonderful chance to visit, with brilliant foliage and cooler temperatures. September and October are great months to visit to stay away from the hordes of the late spring months. Despite the fact that the weather can be erratic, you can still participate in outdoor activities like cycling and hiking. Fall is likewise an incredible opportunity to encounter Estonia's culinary scene, with numerous cafés offering good occasional dishes.

Winter (December to February):

Even though it's cold and snowy in Estonia in the winter, it can be a magical time to visit if you like winter sports and holiday celebrations. The country has numerous ski resorts, and ice skating in Tallinn's central square is a popular pastime. Also worth seeing are the Christmas markets in Tallinn, where you can buy warm drinks, traditional foods, and handmade crafts. In December, there are only about six hours of daylight, so bring warm clothing and plan activities inside as well.

March through May:

The landscape in Estonia comes back to life in the spring, making it a beautiful time to visit. The weather can be unpredictably cold on some days, but it can also be sunny and warm on others. Visit Estonia's national parks in the spring for a chance to see wildflowers and birds on their way south. The Tallinn Music Week festival, which showcases the country's vibrant music scene, also occurs in the spring.

Ultimately, the best time to visit Estonia depends on the things you want to see and do. Assuming you need warm climate and outside exercises, visit throughout the mid year months. If you have any desire to keep away from groups and experience Estonia's occasional cooking, visit in the fall. Visit during the winter months if you enjoy winter sports and holiday celebrations. Visit Estonia in the spring to experience its music scene and witness the landscape's rebirth following the winter. Anything that season you visit, Estonia brings something to the table for everybody.

Visa and passport requirements

For international travel, you need a passport and a visa. They are the primary forms of identification that permit legal travel to other nations.

A permit issued by a foreign government allows travelers to enter and remain in the country for a predetermined amount of time. A visa is an authority report given by an explorer's nation of origin, permitting them to globally travel.

The essential details regarding the requirements for passports and visas will be discussed in this guide.

1 Visa Prerequisites:

For international travel, a passport is essential. It permits legal foreign entry because it serves as proof of identity and citizenship. The following are essential requirements for every traveler's passport:

a. Accuracy: Beyond the intended duration of the traveler's stay in a foreign country, a passport should be valid for at least six months. A few nations might require a more broadened legitimacy period.

b. Page blanks: At least two blank pages for entry and exit stamps should be on a passport.

c. Recharging: If you intend to travel internationally, you must renew your passport before it expires. It's best to submit an application well in advance because the renewal process can take several weeks.

2. Requirements for a Visa:

A permit issued by a foreign government allows travelers to enter and remain in the country for a predetermined amount of time. Visa necessities change by country and rely upon the explorer's citizenship, the motivation behind their visit, and the length of their visit. Every traveler ought to be aware of the essential visa requirements listed below:

a. Visa type: Visas include tourist, business, student, and work visas among others. The purpose of the traveler's visit determines the type of visa required.

B. The Process For Applying: Travelers typically need to submit an application form, passport-size photographs, and supporting documents, such as an invitation letter, proof of financial support, and a trip itinerary in order to submit a visa application.

c. Time to process: Visa handling times fluctuate by country and can require a little while or even a long time now and again. Applying well in advance of your intended travel dates is essential.

3. Authorization for Electronic Travel (ETA):

An electronic travel authorization (ETA) instead of a visa is required in some nations. An electronic document known as an ETA grants travelers temporary entry to the country. It is similar to a visa but does not require a passport stamp. The estimated time of arrival application process is normally quicker and less muddled than a visa application.

4. Travel With No Visa:

Certain nationalities can travel to certain countries without a visa, allowing them to enter the country for a predetermined amount of time. The length of stay fluctuates by country and can go from a couple of days to a while.

Taking everything into account, visa and identification prerequisites are fundamental for global travel. The requirements for obtaining a visa and a passport should be researched well in advance of the travel dates that are planned for the destination. It is absolutely necessary to apply for the necessary visa or ETA and to ensure that your passport is valid and contains sufficient blank pages. Travelers can have a stress-free and enjoyable trip abroad with the right preparation.

Estonia Travel Insurance Guide.

On the off chance that you're arranging an outing to Estonia, it's fundamental to have head out protection to safeguard yourself against unexpected occasions and crises.

What Estonia travel insurance covers, how to buy it, and what to look for in a policy are all covered in this comprehensive guide.

1. What is covered by Estonia travel insurance?

Estonia travel protection regularly covers the accompanying:

i. Medical costs: This takes care of the expense of clinical treatment and hospitalization in the event of sickness or injury during your outing.

Ii. Evacuation for medical emergencies: In the event of a medical emergency, this covers the cost of getting to a medical facility.

Iii. Cancellation or interruption of a trip: If you have to cancel or shorten your trip due to unforeseen circumstances like illness, injury, or death, this will cover the cost.

Iv Lost or taken things: This takes care of the expense of supplanting your lost or taken stuff or individual effects during your outing.

v. Travel delay: This takes care of the expense of extra costs like convenience and food assuming that your outing is deferred because of unanticipated occasions like terrible climate or strikes.

How do I purchase travel insurance for Estonia?

There are multiple ways of buying travel protection for Estonia:

i. **On the web**: Travel insurance can be purchased online from a reputable insurance company. Try to look at strategies and read the fine print prior to making a buy.

ii **Through A Travel Planner**: Travel insurance may be offered as an additional service by a travel agent when you book your trip.

iii **Using a credit card**: Check with the company that issues your credit card to see if you are eligible for travel insurance, which is a benefit of some cards.

What to search for in Estonia travel insurance contract?

When purchasing Estonia travel insurance, be sure to look for the following features:

1 **Assurance**: Check to see that the policy covers everything you need, like medical bills, an emergency evacuation, and having your trip canceled or rescheduled.

2 **Restrictions Imposed By The Policy**: Try to check as far as possible to guarantee that you have sufficient inclusion for your requirements.

3.**Omissions**: Peruse the fine print cautiously to comprehend what isn't covered by the arrangement.

4 **Conditions**: Check to see if the policy covers any pre-existing medical conditions you may have.

5 **Time frame of coverage**: Check to see if the policy covers your entire trip.

6 **Price**: Compare policies to determine which offers the best value.

What additional advice do you have for purchasing travel insurance to Estonia?

Additional advice for purchasing Estonia travel insurance includes the following:

- Buy travel protection when you book your excursion to guarantee inclusion from the outset of your excursion.

- Always keep a copy of your travel insurance policy and your emergency contact information on you.

- If you need to file a claim, get in touch with your insurance company right away to begin the process.

- Be sure to comprehend the claims procedure and the required supporting documentation before filing a claim.

- In the event of a medical emergency, you will be covered if you declare any prior medical conditions.

In conclusion, in order to safeguard yourself from unforeseen circumstances and emergency situations while in Estonia, travel insurance is absolutely necessary. Make a point to look at strategies, comprehend what's covered, and buy a strategy that addresses your issues and spending plan. With the right travel insurance contract, you can experience harmony of the brain and partake in your excursion to Estonia without limit.

Budgeting And Money Matter

When traveling to Estonia, the following is a comprehensive guide to budgeting and money management:

1. **Money Exchange**:

The euro (EUR) is the currency of Estonia. It's prescribed to exchange your money before you show up in Estonia, yet on the off chance that you can't do as such, you can exchange your cash at a bank or cash office. Try not to exchange cash at hotels or air terminals, as they frequently have higher exchange rates.

2. Use Debit And Credit Cards:

The majority of Estonian businesses accept credit and debit cards because the country is highly digitalized. It's prescribed to utilize a Mastercard with no unfamiliar exchange expenses to keep away from additional charges. Even so, it's still a good idea to bring some cash with you to use for smaller purchases.

3 Budget Accommodation

Prices for accommodation in Estonia fluctuate according to location and season. Tallinn, the capital, has a lot of different places to stay, from cheap hostels to expensive hotels. It is advisable to reserve your accommodation in advance if you are traveling during peak season to avoid paying more.

4 Take The Bus Or Train:

Public transportation in Estonia is reasonable and helpful, particularly in Tallinn. The majority of the city's areas are served by the extensive network of buses, trams, and trolleys. Tickets can be purchased from drivers, kiosks, or ticket machines. Additionally, purchasing a Tallinn Card, which provides unlimited access to public transportation and discounts on museums and attractions, is strongly recommended.

5 Dine At Local Eateries:

Estonia has a different culinary scene, and attempting conventional Estonian dishes at nearby restaurants is suggested. Eating at nearby cafés is additionally more reasonable than feasting at touristy spots. For a meal that won't break the bank, look for establishments that have a "lunch menu" or "daily special."

6 Visit Free Attractions:

Parks, museums, and galleries are among the free attractions in Estonia. Kadriorg Park, Toompea Hill, and the Old Town of Tallinn are all free to visit. Additionally, the Kumu Art Museum should be visited because it offers free admission on the last Friday of each month.

7 Arrangement For Journeys:

Estonia offers a variety of excursions, including wildlife viewing, cycling, and hiking. To avoid paying more for excursions, it's best to book them in advance. You can likewise lease bikes in Tallinn to investigate the city at your own speed.

8 Think About Travel Insurance:

While Estonia is a protected country to visit, it's prescribed to buy go protection to safeguard yourself from unexpected conditions. Medical emergencies, trip cancellations, and lost or stolen luggage are all covered by travel insurance.

9 Be Wary Of Tourist Traps:

Estonia has its fair share of tourist traps, just like any other tourist destination. Stay away from cafés with exorbitant costs and forceful promoting strategies, and be careful about road merchants selling modest trinkets. Additionally, avoid tourist-heavy areas during peak hours.

By following these planning and cash the executives tips, you can partake in your outing to Estonia without burning through every last cent.

Chapter 2, Top Destination And Attraction

Estonia is a country with a lot of history and culture. It has a lot of places to visit and attractions. Estonia has something for everyone, from beautiful beaches to medieval cities. Here are a portion of the top attractions and objections of Estonia.

Tallinn Old Town

The medieval Old Town of Tallinn, Estonia's capital, is well-known for its preservation. The Old Town is an UNESCO World Legacy Site and is home to various memorable structures, including the Toompea Palace, St. Olaf's Congregation, and the Municipal center Square. Additionally, there are a number of cafes, restaurants, and shops in the Old Town where tourists can sample traditional Estonian cuisine and purchase souvenirs.

National Park Lahemaa

Lahemaa National Park is a beautiful natural area on Estonia's northern coast that is home to a wide range of animals, including brown bears, lynx, and wolves. Guests to the recreation area can investigate its woodlands, wetlands, and shoreline, and appreciate exercises like climbing, cycling, and fishing.

Tartu

Tartu, the second-largest city in Estonia, is well-known for its stunning architecture, thriving cultural scene, and historic university. The Estonian National Museum, the Tartu Art Museum, and the University of Tartu Museum are just a few of the numerous museums and galleries in Tartu.

Pärnu

Pärnu, which is on the southwestern coast of Estonia, is well-known for its stunning beaches and spa resorts. The town has a long history as a spa destination, and its numerous spas and wellness centers offer treatments like mud baths and massages to visitors. Additionally, Pärnu has a lively nightlife thanks to the numerous bars and clubs that stay open late.

Hiiumaa Island

Hiiumaa is Estonia's second-biggest island, situated off the country's western coast. The island is well-known for its stunning scenery, which includes forests, rocky coastline, and lighthouses. Guests to Hiiumaa can appreciate exercises like climbing, cycling, and fishing, and can likewise investigate the island's numerous noteworthy temples and windmills.

National Park of Soomaa

Soomaa National Park is a stunning natural area in the center of Estonia that is home to a wide range of animals, including otters, elk, and beavers. The park has five distinct seasons, one of which is a "fifth season" of floods in the spring. The park has wetlands, forests, and opportunities for canoeing and hiking for its visitors.

Island of Saaremaa

Estonia's largest island, Saaremaa, can be found just off the country's southwest coast. The island is well-known for its stunning scenery, which includes sandy beaches, lighthouses, and windmills. Activities like hiking, cycling, and fishing can be enjoyed by visitors to Saaremaa, which is known for its numerous historic churches and castles.

Burg Narva:
On the border between Estonia and Russia is the historic Narva Castle. The castle was built in the 13th century and has undergone numerous reconstructions and restorations over the years. It is now home to a museum that tells the story of the castle and the region's history.

Castle Rakvere:
The town of Rakvere in northern Estonia is home to the medieval castle known as Rakvere Castle. The castle, which was built in the 14th century, has been renovated and rebuilt

numerous times over the years. It is now home to a museum that tells the story of the castle and the region's history.

Museum of Kumu Art

The largest art museum in Estonia is the Kumu Art Museum, which is in Tallinn, the capital city. In addition to works by international artists, the museum houses a substantial collection of Estonian art from the medieval period to the present day. The gallery likewise has transitory displays, shows, and other far-reaching developments consistently.

Otepää

Otepää is a small town in the southern part of Estonia that is well-known for its natural beauty and facilities for winter sports. The town is surrounded by forests and lakes that provide opportunities for hiking and fishing, and it is a popular destination for skiing, snowboarding, and other winter sports.

Estonian Outdoors Historical Center

The Estonian Open Air Museum is a one-of-a-kind outdoor museum on the outskirts of Tallinn that documents village life in Estonia from the 18th to the 20th century. Guests to the exhibition hall can investigate conventional Estonian farmhouses, places of worship, and windmills, and find out about the country's provincial history and culture.

Toila:

Toila is a humble community situated on Estonia's northeastern coast, known for its delightful oceanside park and notable Toila Spa. The town is a famous location for unwinding and health, and guests can appreciate medicines like back rubs and hydrotherapy at the spa, or investigate the recreation area's lovely nurseries and shoreline sees.

Paldiski:

Paldiski is a small town on Estonia's northern coast that is famous for its scenic coastal views and historic military sites. Visitors can explore the town's numerous abandoned military buildings and bunkers as well as the nearby Pakri Islands, which offer opportunities for hiking and birdwatching. The town was once an important military port for the Soviet Union.

Lake Peipsi:

Peipsi Lake is an enormous freshwater lake situated on Estonia's eastern boundary, imparted to Russia. The unique culture and cuisine of the lake are rooted in the customs of the local Russian Old Believers community. Guests to the lake can investigate customary Old Adherents towns, test nearby dishes like smoked fish and cured cucumbers, and appreciate exercises like fishing and drifting.

These are only a couple of the numerous attractions and objections that Estonia brings to the table. Estonia has something for everyone, whether you're into history, culture, nature, or relaxation.

Chapter 3: Food And Drink

Estonian Cuisine.

Dishes of fish:

Fish dishes are an important part of Estonian cuisine because of the country's location along the coast. The most famous fish dishes incorporate smoked or seared Baltic herring, eel soup, and salted Baltic herring. The smoked fish is ordinarily presented with sharp cream and bubbled potatoes, while the eel soup is made with cream, onions, and potatoes.

Dishes for meat:

Pork and hamburger are the most generally eaten meats in Estonian cooking. Sausage, pork chop, and pork roast are all made with pork. Stews and meatballs usually contain beef. Blood sausage (), made with barley, pork blood, and spices, is a well-liked traditional meat dish.

Potatoes:

Potatoes are a staple food in Estonian cooking and are utilized in numerous conventional dishes. They are in many cases bubbled or pounded and filled in as a side dish. Potato salad, which consists of boiled potatoes, mayonnaise, and pickles, is one popular potato dish.

Kohupiim

Estonian cuisine relies heavily on dairy products. Harsh cream, buttermilk, and cheddar are usually utilized in dishes. Kohupiim, a kind of curd cheese that is used to make pastries and desserts, is one traditional dairy product.

Bread:

Bread is a staple of Estonian cuisine, and the country produces numerous varieties of bread. Rye bread is the most famous sort of bread and is regularly dim and thick. Different sorts of bread incorporate white bread, wheat bread, and grain bread.

Soups:

Soups are a well known piece of Estonian cooking and are many times filled in as a principal course. One well known soup is pea soup, which is made with dried peas, pork, and vegetables. Mushroom soup, which is made with fresh mushrooms and cream, is another popular soup.

Desserts:

Estonian treats are normally sweet and frequently contain organic products. Kama, a sweet porridge made from roasted barley, rye, wheat, and pea flour, is one popular dessert. Another well known treat is apple cake, which is made with apples, cinnamon, and a sweet baked good covering.

Beverages:

In Estonia, beer is the most widely consumed alcoholic beverage, and there are numerous varieties of Estonian beers. Vana Tallinn, a sweet liqueur made with rum and a variety of spices, is another widely consumed alcoholic beverage. Kefir, a drink made with sour milk, and kvass, a rye bread-based fermented beverage, are examples of non-alcoholic beverages.

Top Estonian Dishes To Try

Dark bread, or leib in Estonian, is a staple food in Estonian cooking. Rye flour is used to make this dense, dark bread with a flavor that is slightly sweet and tangy. It is an essential component of Estonian cuisine and is frequently accompanied by fish, cheese, or butter.

Kohuke

Kohuke is a popular Estonian snack with a chocolate-covered sweet cream cheese filling. This tasty treat is a number one among local people and is many times delighted in as a late morning bite or sweet.

Mulgipuder

The Mulgi region of Estonia is home to the traditional Estonian dish known as Mulgipuder.

It is a hearty porridge made of potatoes and barley that is typically accompanied by bacon and onions. This dish is great for cold winter days because of its rich, smoky flavor.

Blood sausage, also known as verivorstid, is a traditional Estonian sausage made from barley and blood from pork. It is frequently presented with lingonberry jam and sauerkraut and is a well known dish during Christmas and other merry events.

The traditional Estonian flour mixture known as kama

kama is made from roasted barley, rye, wheat, peas, and other grains. It is frequently combined with milk, yogurt, or kefir for breakfast or dessert. Kama is a favorite among Estonians because of its slightly nutty and sweet flavor.

Kiluvileib
Kiluvileib, also known as a sprat sandwich, is a popular snack in Estonia that typically consists of black bread and sprats, which are small fish. The sprats are generally marinated in oil,

vinegar, and flavors and are served on top of the bread with onions and acrid cream.

Rosolje

Rosolje is a conventional Estonian plate of mixed greens that is ordinarily made with beets, potatoes, herring, and sharp cream. Estonians adore this vibrant salad, which is well-known for its sweet and sour flavor.

Baking soda, buttermilk, and rye flour are used to make the traditional Estonian flatbread known as karask. It is a staple in Estonian cuisine and is typically accompanied by cheese, honey, or butter.

The traditional Estonian soup

known as kapsasupp, or cabbage soup, is made with cabbage, potatoes, carrots, and occasionally pork. The Estonians love this hearty soup, which is often served with black bread.

Räim

Räim, or Baltic herring, is a little, sleek fish that is a number one among Estonians. It is typically eaten with black bread, potatoes, and sour cream and is frequently smoked or marinated.

Best Restaurants In Estonia

There are a lot of restaurants in the country that serve a wide range of cuisines, from traditional Estonian fare to international fare. We'll look at some of Estonia's best restaurants in this guide.

Contemporary Estonian cuisine

Tallinn's Old Town is home to a fine-dining establishment called. Contemporary Estonian cuisine is on the menu at the restaurant, with a focus on seasonal and locally sourced ingredients. The dishes are wonderfully introduced, and the assistance is faultless. The restaurant, which has a Michelin star and is one of the most popular places to eat in Estonia, is one of the best.

The waterfront restaurant NOA

NOA is just outside of Tallinn in the suburb of Pirita. The café offers staggering perspectives on the Baltic Ocean and serves a blend of contemporary and conventional Estonian cooking. The restaurant is known for its seafood dishes that are made with the freshest ingredients and has a large wine list.

Rataskaevu 16
Rataskaevu 16 is a cozy, rustic restaurant in the Old Town of Tallinn. The menu changes frequently to reflect the best ingredients of the season, and it serves traditional Estonian cuisine with a modern twist. The restaurant has a warm and welcoming atmosphere and is popular with both locals and tourists.

The farm-to-table restaurant

Leib Resto ja Aed can be found in Tallinn's trendy Kalamaja neighborhood. The restaurant serves a mix of contemporary and traditional Estonian cuisine and gets its ingredients from farms and producers in the area. On a sunny day, the restaurant's lovely garden terrace is a great spot to eat.

Tchaikovsky

Tchaikovsky is a Russian top notch café situated in the Swissotel in Tallinn. The menu includes classic dishes like caviar, blinis, and borscht, as well as a mix of Russian and French cuisine. The decor is grand and elegant, and the service is excellent.

Phjaka

Phjaka is a guesthouse and restaurant outside of Tallinn in the countryside. The menu changes frequently to reflect the best ingredients of the season and serves rustic Estonian cuisine. The café is housed in a perfectly reestablished stable and has a comfortable and private environment.

F-hoone

F-hoone is a relaxed and popular eatery situated in the Kalamaja neighborhood of Tallinn. The café serves a blend of Estonian and global cooking, and the menu highlights burgers, pizzas, and mixed greens. The restaurant has a laid-back and relaxed atmosphere and is popular with young people.

Kohvik Sesoon

is a charming cafe in the heart of Tallinn's Old Town. Kohvik Sesoon is cozy and charming. The bistro serves a blend of customary and current Estonian food, and the menu changes much of the time to mirror the season's best fixings. The bistro is known for its hand crafted cakes and baked goods and has a wonderful outside porch.

Restoran Juur
is a fine-dining establishment in the town of Tartu in the southern part of Estonia. The menu at the restaurant includes items like smoked eel, wild boar, and spruce shoots, which are a combination of traditional and contemporary Estonian cuisine. The restaurant is a great place to experience Estonian hospitality and has a warm and inviting atmosphere.

Meat Market

Meat Market is an easygoing and popular café situated in the Rotermann Quarter of Tallinn. Steaks, burgers, and other grilled meats are on the menu at the restaurant, which specializes in meat dishes. The café likewise offers veggie lovers and vegetarian choices. The environment is exuberant, and the café has an extraordinary choice of specialty lagers and mixed drinks.

Tallinn's Pirita Neighborhood

is home to the elegant restaurant Tuljak. The eatery offers shocking perspectives on the ocean and serves a blend of Estonian and European cooking. Lamb, seafood, and homemade pasta are all on the menu. The restaurant is a great spot for a special occasion thanks to its contemporary and sophisticated decor.

F-hoone Kohvik

The cafe and restaurant F-hoone Kohvik

can be found in Tallinn's Kalamaja neighborhood. The eatery serves a blend of Estonian and worldwide food, and the menu highlights dishes like barbecued fish, mixed greens, and sandwiches. The bistro has a relaxed and easygoing environment, and the outside seating region is an incredible put to partake in a dinner on a radiant day.

Art Priori

The fine-dining establishment Art Priori can be found in the center of Tallinn's Old Town. The menu at the restaurant includes items like venison, elk tartare, and beetroot risotto, all of which are modern interpretations of Estonian cuisine. The restaurant is a great spot for a romantic dinner or a special occasion because of its contemporary and sophisticated decor.

Rucola Rucola

The Italian restaurant Rucola Rucola is in Tallinn's Rotermann Quarter. The eatery serves real Italian cooking, and the menu highlights dishes like pizza, pasta, and risotto. The restaurant is a great spot for a meal with friends or family because of its warm and inviting atmosphere.

Tallinn's Kalamaja

Tallinn's Kalamaja neighborhood is home to the Japanese eatery Umami Umami. Sushi, sashimi, and tempura are just a few of the authentic Japanese dishes on the menu at the restaurant.

The eatery has a cutting edge and moderate style, and the help is incredible.

Estonian Drinks

Estonian drinks are no special case, offering many heavenly refreshments that are popular with the two local people and sightseers. In this article, we'll explore likely the most renowned Estonian drinks, including alcoholic and non-alcoholic decisions.

Kali

Kali is a non-mixed drink that is outstandingly popular in Estonia. It tastes marginally harsh and is produced using rye bread that has been aged. Kali is likewise utilized as a base for mixed drinks and is as often as possible drunk as an invigorating refreshment on warm mid year days.

Vana Tallinn,

Vana Tallinn, which has been created in Estonia starting around 1960, is a popular alcohol. Rum, vanilla, citrus oils, and various different flavors and flavorings are utilized to make it. Vana Tallinn has a rich, sweet taste and is regularly gotten a kick out of as a digestif after a supper.

Mix

Ale is a particularly notable mixed drink in Estonia, with a strong maturing custom returning many years. Saku, A. Le Coq, and Phjala are a couple of the most popular lagers created in Estonia. Estonian brew is famous with customary Estonian dishes like dark bread, smoked meat, and salted vegetables as a result of its fresh, invigorating flavor.

Kännu Kukk

Kännu Kukk is solid areas for an ale that is matured in the town of Viljandi. It has a rich, malty flavor and a high alcohol content, making it a main among blend darlings.

Mead

Mead is a honey-based mixed drink that has been popular in Estonia for quite a while. It tastes sweet and floral and is made by maturing honey with water, flavors, and flavorings. Mead is much of the time consumed at celebrations and other conventional Estonian festivals.

vodka

In Estonia, vodka is a famous cocktail that is oftentimes consumed as a shot or in mixed drinks. Viru Valge and Saaremaa Vodka are among the most notable Estonian vodka brands. It is notable that Estonian vodka is unadulterated and tastes smooth.

Kaseke

A customary Estonian alcohol produced using birch buds is called Kaseke. It is as often as possible consumed as a digestif and has a sweet, botanical flavor. Mixed drinks and treats likewise contain kaseke as a seasoning.

Muhu Leib

Muhu Leib is a unique Estonian alcohol made with flavors and flavorings from dark bread. It is oftentimes consumed as a digestif or as an enhancing in mixed drinks and has a rich, hearty flavor.

Chapter 4: Accommodation in Estonia

Best Places To Stay In Estonia.

Tallinn

Tallinn, on Estonia's north coast, is both the country's capital and largest city. The well-preserved medieval old town, cobblestone streets, and ancient city walls make it a UNESCO World Heritage Site. Tallinn has a lot of different places to stay, from cheap hostels to expensive hotels. Guests can choose a more contemporary hotel in the city center or stay in the heart of the old town.

Tartu

Estonia's second-largest city is Tartu, which is in the country's southeast. It is well-known for its theaters, museums, galleries, and university town status. Tartu has a lot of options for lodging, from guesthouses to hotels. In the city center or in the quieter suburbs, visitors can stay.

Pärnu

Pärnu is a resort town on Estonia's southwest coast that is well-known for its spa resorts and sandy beaches. Especially during the summer, it is a popular tourist destination. In Pärnu, there are a lot of places to stay, from cheap hostels to expensive hotels. In the city center or in the quieter suburbs, visitors can stay.

Saaremaa

Estonia's largest island, Saaremaa, can be found in the Baltic Sea. Because of its natural beauty, historic sites, and cultural heritage, it is a popular tourist destination. On Saaremaa, you can stay in a variety of places, from guesthouses to hotels. On the island, visitors can stay in Kuressaare, the capital, or in one of the many smaller towns and villages.

Lahemaa

Lahemaa National Park The forest, wetlands, and coastal areas of Lahemaa National Park, which is in the north of Estonia, are among its many distinctive landscapes. In the park or in the nearby town of Rakvere, guests can stay in a variety of guesthouses and cottages.

Hiiumaa

In the Baltic Sea, Hiiumaa is the second-largest island in Estonia. It is well-known for its natural beauty, cultural heritage, and historic sites. On the island or in the town of Kärdla, there are numerous guesthouses and cottages for rent.

Otepää

Otepää is a humble community situated in southern Estonia, known for its colder time of year sports offices and normal excellence. Guests can remain in one of the numerous guesthouses and bungalows situated in the town, or in the close-by city of Tartu.

Hotels, Hostels And Guesthouses

There are different convenience choices accessible in Estonia, going from financial plan agreeable lodgings to rich lodgings. Here is a thorough manual for the various sorts of facilities accessible in Estonia, alongside their assessed costs:

Lodgings:

Lodgings are the most financial plan accommodating convenience choice in Estonia. They offer dorm style rooms with lofts and shared washrooms. A few inns likewise offer confidential rooms with ensuite washrooms. The typical expense for a bed in a lodging dorm is between €10-€20 each evening. Confidential rooms start from €30 each evening.

Guesthouses:
Guesthouses are a famous convenience choice in Estonia. They offer confidential rooms with shared or ensuite washrooms. A few guesthouses likewise have kitchen offices for visitors to utilize. The typical expense for a twofold room in a guesthouse is between €30-€50 each evening.

Lofts:
Condos are an extraordinary choice for voyagers who need a more private and agreeable stay. They offer completely prepared kitchens, confidential washrooms, and living spaces. The typical expense for a one-room condo in Estonia is between €40-€80 each evening.

Inns:
Estonia has a scope of lodgings to suit all spending plans and inclinations. From spending plan agreeable choices to rich five-star inns, there is something for everybody. The typical expense for a twofold room in a three-star lodging is between €50-€100 each evening, while five-star lodgings can cost upwards of €200 each evening.

Shop inns:

Store lodgings offer an interesting and customized insight for voyagers. They are in many cases more modest and more cozy than customary lodgings, with an emphasis on plan and style. The typical expense for a twofold room in a shop lodging is between €100-€200 each evening.

Visitor condos:

Visitor lofts are an incredible choice for families or gatherings of companions voyaging together. They offer completely prepared kitchens, various rooms, and living spaces. The typical expense for a two-room visitor loft is between €80-€150 each evening.

Setting Up Camp

Setting up camp is a well known choice for outside lovers in Estonia. There are numerous camping areas all through the nation, offering offices like showers, latrines, and outing regions. The typical expense for a tent to contribute to a campground is between €10-€20 each evening.

Estonia has a scope of convenience choices to suit all financial plans and inclinations. Whether you're searching for a financial plan accommodating an inn or a sumptuous store inn, you're certain to track down the ideal spot to remain in this gorgeous country.

How to Get a Room in Estonia

There are a few different ways to get a room in Estonia, depending on your preferences and how much money you have. Here are the absolute most normal techniques:

1 Online Booking Sites

In Estonia, booking websites provide a diverse selection of lodging options. To find the ideal hotel, you can narrow your search b y price, location, and amenities.

2 Direct Reservation

In Estonia, a lot of hotels, guesthouses, and apartments have their own websites where you can make a direct reservation. If you want to talk to the owner or manager directly and negotiate prices, this might be a good choice.

3 Travel Firms:

If you book a package tour to Estonia, your travel agent probably will book your lodging on your behalf. If you want everything taken care of at once, this might be a good choice.

When planning your trip to Estonia, the lodging you choose is a crucial factor. Estonia has something for everyone, whether you're looking for a luxurious hotel, a cozy guesthouse, or a hostel that's affordable. To ensure that you have a pleasant and comfortable stay, research the location, amenities, and reviews prior to making a reservation for your lodging.

It's also important to think about when you'll be in Estonia because it can affect prices and availability. Top season is regularly from June to August, when the weather conditions are hottest and numerous celebrations and occasions occur. With fewer people and lower prices, shoulder season (May and September) can be a good value.

It's a good idea to book your lodging in advance, especially during peak seasons when there may be limited availability. On the other hand, if you travel during the off-season, you might be able to get last-minute deals or directly negotiate prices with the manager or owner.

Airbnb options in Estonia

Tallinn, the capital city of Estonia, is a well known destination for vacationers. The city's Old Town is an UNESCO World Legacy Site, with middle age design, cobbled roads, and a lively nightlife.

There are numerous Airbnb choices accessible in Tallinn, going from comfortable condos to memorable apartments.

On the off chance that you're searching for a remarkable encounter, consider remaining in one of Tallinn's middle age towers, for example, the Paks Margareeta tower, which has been changed over into an open loft with perspectives on the Old Town. Another choice is the "Katarina Pinnacle Suite," which is situated in a fourteenth century tower in the core of the city.

Notwithstanding Tallinn, there are numerous other enchanting towns and urban communities to investigate in Estonia. Tartu, the second-biggest city in Estonia, is known for its energetic understudy populace and noteworthy college. There are numerous Airbnb choices accessible in Tartu, including comfortable condos and extensive estates.

On the off chance that you're searching for an ocean side get-away, consider visiting the retreat town of Pärnu, which is situated on the bank of the Baltic Ocean. There are numerous Airbnb choices accessible in Pärnu, going from comfortable houses to roomy condos with ocean views.

For nature darlings, Estonia has numerous public stops and woodlands to investigate. Lahemaa Public Park, situated on the northern bank of Estonia, is a well known objective for climbing, cycling, and untamed life watching. There are numerous Airbnb choices accessible in the close-by towns of Käsmu and Võsu, including comfortable lodges and extensive manors.

Chapter 5: Activities and things to do in Estonia

Hiking and trekking

One such movement is climbing and journeying, which is turning out to be progressively famous among local people and sightseers. Estonia has a wide range of landscapes for hikers and trekkers to explore, including its picturesque coastline, dense forests, and tranquil lakes. We will provide you with a comprehensive guide to hiking and trekking in Estonia in this article.

The best time to hike and trek in Estonia is:

Between the end of spring and the beginning of autumn (May to October), hiking and trekking in Estonia are at their best. The landscapes are vibrant with wildflowers and greenery during this time of mild and dry weather. However, since weather conditions can change rapidly, it is essential to check the weather forecast before going on a trip.

Top Estonian Trekking and Hiking Trails:

Lahemaa Public Park:

Lahemaa National Park is Estonia's largest national park, covering 725 square kilometers and being on the country's northern coast. There are a number of hiking trails in the park, one of which is the 4-kilometer-long Viru Bog trail, which takes you through a stunning landscape of peat bogs.

Soomaa Public Park:

Soomaa Public Park is situated in southern Estonia and covers an area of 390 square kilometers. The recreation area is known for its broad wetlands, waterways, and floodplains, making it an astounding objective for nature sweethearts. Because it affords breathtaking views of the surrounding landscapes, the three-kilometer Riisa hiking trail is a popular choice for hikers.

National Park of Matsalu:

The 486-square-kilometer Matsalu National Park can be found in western Estonia. The park is well-known for its diverse birdlife, and the best times to visit are during the spring and fall migrations of birds. The scenic views of the river and its surroundings make the 6-kilometer Kasari River trail a popular choice for hikers.

Nature Park Otepää:

Otepää Nature Park is situated in southern Estonia and covers an area of 22 square kilometers. The park is great for hiking and trekking because of its rolling hills and thick forests. Hikers frequently take the 6-kilometer Lake Pühajärv trail because it affords breathtaking views of the lake and its surroundings.

Phja-Krvemaa National Park:

The130-square-kilometer Phja-Krvemaa Nature Reserve is situated in northern Estonia. The save is known for its tough scenes and thick woodlands, making it a superb objective for explorers and adventurers. With stunning views of the peat bog and its surroundings, the 8-kilometer Viru Bog trail is a popular choice for hikers.

Safety Tips for Estonian Hiking and Trekking:

Wear Fitting Apparel And Footwear: The climate in Estonia can be unusual, so wearing fitting apparel and footwear for the conditions is fundamental.

Convey Sufficient Food And Water: Make sure you bring enough water and food with you for the hike or trek. It is likewise smart to convey a water decontamination framework on the off chance that you run out of water.

Know Your Cutoff Points: Choose a hiking or trekking trail that is appropriate for your experience and fitness level. It's also important to take breaks when they're needed and not work too hard.

Actually take a look at the weather conditions estimate: Look at the weather conditions figure prior to heading on a climb or trip, and be ready for changes in weather patterns.

Take the marked routes: Stay on the marked trails and avoid venturing into uncharted territory as this can be risky and raise the likelihood of becoming lost or injured.

Carry A Compass And Map: Know how to use a map and compass to navigate the trails and always carry them with you.

Tell Somebody Your Arrangements: Inform someone of your plans before going on a hike or trek, including the route you intend to take, your anticipated arrival time, and emergency contact information.

Be Kind To Nature: Respecting nature and leaving no trace is essential because Estonia is home to numerous ecosystems and species of wildlife. Be sure to properly dispose of waste to avoid harming animals and plants.

Know About Expected Perils: Know about possible perils, like steep drops, elusive rocks, and hazardous natural life, and play it safe.

Have A First Aid Kit On You: Always keep a first aid kit with essential medical supplies like bandages, antiseptics, and painkillers on hand.

Cycling

Cycling is a famous open air movement in Estonia, a little Northern European nation situated on the eastern bank of the Baltic Ocean. Estonia is known for its delightful open country, timberlands, lakes, and a long shore, which gives an optimal setting to cycling devotees.

Cycling Foundation In Estonia

Estonia has an advanced cycling foundation, with committed bicycle ways and paths in urban communities and towns. Lately, the public authority has put resources into growing the cycling framework to make it more secure and more helpful for cyclists. The nation has in excess of 2,000 kilometers of checked cycling courses, and the majority of them are cleared and signposted. A portion of the famous cycling courses in Estonia are:

Tartu - Valga cycling course:

This 130-kilometer course begins from the college town of Tartu and goes through the wonderful wide open of Southern Estonia to the town of Valga on the Latvian boundary. The course goes through a few little towns and towns and offers shocking perspectives on woods, lakes, and streams.

Tallinn - Pärnu cycling course:

This 120-kilometer course begins from the capital city of Tallinn and goes through the seaside towns of Northern Estonia to the hotel town of Pärnu. The course offers delightful perspectives on the Baltic Ocean and goes through a few notable destinations and milestones.

Haapsalu - Rohuküla cycling course: This 50-kilometer course begins from the ocean side town of Haapsalu and goes through the grand field of Western Estonia to the ship port of Rohuküla. The course goes through a few little towns and offers staggering perspectives on the shore and the ocean.

Cycling occasions in Estonia:

Estonia has a few cycling occasions consistently, going from sporting rides to cutthroat races. A portion of the well known cycling occasions in Estonia are:

Tartu Rattaralli:

This is the biggest cycling occasion in the nation, held every year in May. The occasion draws in a great many cyclists from everywhere Estonia and adjoining nations and offers a few distance choices, going from 40 kilometers to 135 kilometers.

Estonia Visit:

This is an expert cycling race held every year in June, highlighting a portion of the top groups and riders from around the world. The race covers in excess of 1,000 kilometers north of a few phases, with the beginning and finish in the capital city of Tallinn.

Visit Through Estonia:

This is a UCI classification 2.1 expert cycling race held every year in August. The race covers in excess of 500 kilometers north of four phases, with the beginning and finish in various towns and urban communities across Estonia.

Ways to cycle in Estonia:

Look at the weather conditions gauge prior to heading, as the climate in Estonia can be erratic.

Wear fitting dress and stuff, particularly during the colder months, when temperatures can decrease underneath freezing.

Bring a lot of water and bites, as there may not be many spots to purchase food and beverages along the cycling courses.

Adhere to the traffic guidelines and signs, and be aware of other street clients, including walkers and vehicles.

Enjoy reprieves and partake in the landscape, as cycling in Estonia offers staggering perspectives on the open country and the shore.

Skiing And Snowboarding

Estonia is as yet a famous destination for skiing and snowboarding lovers because of its advanced winter sports foundation and various ski resorts.

Skiing and snowboarding in Estonia Despite its relatively flat terrain, the country still provides numerous opportunities for these sports. A large portion of the ski resorts in Estonia are situated in the southeastern piece of the nation, close to the line with Russia, where the scene is marginally uneven. In Estonia, the ski season typically begins toward the end of November and lasts until early April.

Estonian ski resorts The following are some of Estonia's most well-known ski resorts:

The largest and most well-known ski resort in Estonia is the Otepää Ski Resort, which is in the town of Otepää. It has cross-country skiing trails and a variety of slopes for skiers and snowboarders of all levels. The retreat likewise includes a ski school, gear rental, and a few eateries and bistros.

The Väike-Munamäe Ski Resort has five slopes of varying difficulty levels and is located in the southeast of Estonia. The hotel likewise has a snow park for snowboarding lovers, as well as a ski school and gear rental.

Kivi'li Adventure Centre - Kivi'li is best known for its motocross and karting tracks, but it also has a small ski resort with two slopes where you can ski and snowboard. The retreat likewise has a snow park with rails and hops for free-form skiing and snowboarding.

Haanja Ski Resort is well-known for its picturesque landscape and well-maintained ski slopes. It is close to the town of Vru. In addition to tracks for cross-country skiing, the resort has seven slopes for skiing and snowboarding.

Skiing and snowboarding lessons for beginners are available at the majority of Estonia's ski resorts. Most of the time, certified instructors lead the lessons, which cover the fundamentals of skiing and snowboarding like safety, how to use the equipment, and technique. Hardware rental is likewise accessible at the greater part of the ski resorts.

Cross-country skiing There are numerous tracks and trails for both recreational and competitive cross-country skiing in Estonia, making it a popular winter sport. The Otepää World Cup track, which is used for international competitions, is the cross-country skiing track that is most well-known in Estonia.

Water Sports In Estonia.

Estonia offers an assortment of water sports exercises for guests to appreciate. In this article, we will investigate probably the most famous water sports in Estonia.

Cruising and Drifting

Cruising and drifting are famous water sports in Estonia, because of the country's longshore and various lakes and streams. Estonia has in excess of 2,000 islands, a considerable lot of which are uninhabited, making it an ideal area for mariners and boaters searching for an experience. Estonia has a rich history of cruising and has delivered numerous elite mariners.

Paddling and Kayaking

Estonia's waterways and lakes offer magnificent open doors for paddling and kayaking. The nation has north of 1,500 waterways and in excess of 1,000 lakes, making it an optimal objective for rowing aficionados. The Soomaa Public Park, situated in the south of the nation, is a famous objective for paddling and kayaking, because of its various waterways and wetlands.

Windsurfing

Windsurfing is a famous water sport in Estonia, because of the country's blustery circumstances. The waterfront areas of Estonia offer superb circumstances for windsurfing, with waves arriving at up to two meters in level. The blustery season in Estonia begins in May and goes on until October, making it an extraordinary objective for windsurfing fans.

Kitesurfing

Kitesurfing is a moderately new water sport in Estonia, however it has in short order acquired prevalence among local people and vacationers. The country's blustery circumstances make it an optimal objective for kitesurfing, with the best spots situated on the northern coast. The season for kitesurfing in Estonia is from May to October.

Stand-Up Paddleboarding

Stand-up paddleboarding (SUP) is a tomfoolery and simple water sport that is acquiring prevalence in Estonia. The nation's lakes and waterways give quiet and picturesque spots to paddleboarding. The SUP season in Estonia begins in May and goes on until October.

Fishing

Fishing is a famous diversion in Estonia, because of the country's wealth of lakes, waterways, and shoreline. Guests can look for different types of fish, including pike, roost, and salmon. A fishing grant is expected to fish in Estonia, which can be gotten from nearby specialists or on the web.

Swimming

Swimming is a famous water movement in Estonia, with the country's shore offering numerous superb sea shores for swimming. Also, Estonia has numerous normal swimming spots, including lakes and waterways. Guests can swim in the Baltic Ocean, yet it is vital to take note that the water can be cool, even in the mid-year months.

Cultural Events And Festivals

Tallinn Old Town Days:

Tallinn Old Town Days is a social celebration that happens every year in the capital city of Tallinn. The celebration commends the city's rich history and culture by exhibiting conventional music, dance, food, and artworks. Guests can partake in directed visits, road exhibitions, and different far-reaching developments that occur all through the city.

Weekend Festival at Parnu:

The Parnu Weekend Celebration is a famous summer celebration that happens in the beachfront city of Parnu. With street food, craft markets, and a variety of music and dance performances, the festival celebrates Estonian culture. Beach volleyball, paddleboarding, and kayaking are just a few of the outdoor pursuits available to visitors.

Hanseatic Days in Tartu:

The annual cultural festival known as the Tartu Hanseatic Days is held in the city of Tartu. With various music and dance performances, historical reenactments, and craft markets, the festival commemorates the city's medieval history as well as its Hanseatic heritage. Traditional Estonian cuisine and guided tours of the city's historic landmarks are also available to visitors.

Festival of Folk Music in Viljandi:

The Viljandi Society Live performance is a well known live concert that happens every year in the town of Viljandi. The festival features performances by local and international artists to celebrate Estonian traditional music and dance. Guests can likewise participate in studios and workshops on customary music and dance.

Tallinn's Christmas Marketplace:

A well-liked winter festival, the Christmas Market in Tallinn takes place in the capital city of Tallinn. Christmas-themed activities like music and dance performances, craft fairs, and traditional food stalls are part of the festival's holiday celebrations. Ice skating and other outdoor activities are also available to visitors.

Festival of Black Nights Films:

Tallinn hosts an annual international film festival known as the Black Nights Film Festival. Films from all over the world, including feature films, documentaries, and shorts, are shown at the festival. Seminars and workshops on various aspects of filmmaking are also available to visitors.

Estonian Routine Celebration:

Every five years in Tallinn, the Estonian Song and Dance Festival is a national cultural event. The festival features a variety of music and dance performances by local and international artists to celebrate Estonian culture. Thousands of performers take part in a mass choir and dance performance at the festival's conclusion.

Chapter 6 :Practical Information For Travelers

Currency And Money

Estonia has a cutting edge and advanced money and monetary framework. The nation has embraced advanced innovation, and e-installments are turning out to be progressively well known. The Euro is the authority money, and most exchanges are credit only. The country's monetary foundations offer a scope of items and administrations, and ATMs are inescapable. Generally speaking, Estonia's cash and cash framework is proficient, secure, and simple to utilize.

Cash in Estonia:

The money in Estonia is the Euro (EUR), which supplanted the Estonian Kroon (EEK) in 2011. The reception of the Euro was a huge step for Estonia, as it was the primary country in the previous Soviet Association to take on the Euro as its true cash. The Euro is presently the authority cash of 19 European Patron states, including Estonia.

Banknotes and coins:

The Euro is separated into banknotes and coins. The banknotes come in sections of €5, €10, €20, €50, €100, €200, and €500. The coins are accessible in eight sections: 1 penny, 2 pennies, 5 pennies, a dime, 20 pennies, 50 pennies, €1, and €2. The plan of Estonian Euro coins mirrors the nation's set of experiences, culture, and nature.

Installment frameworks:

Estonia has a cutting edge and advanced installment framework, and most exchanges are credit only. Bank moves, card installments, and versatile installments are famous installment techniques in the country. Estonians have embraced computerized innovation, and e-installments are turning out to be progressively famous. Many banks in Estonia offer web based financial administrations, which make it simpler for individuals to deal with their funds.

Monetary foundations:

There are a few monetary foundations in Estonia, including business banks, credit associations, and reserve funds banks. The biggest business banks in Estonia are Swedbank, SEB, LHV, and Danske Bank. These banks offer a scope of monetary items and administrations, including credits, investment accounts, and speculation items. The Bank of Estonia is the country's national bank, answerable for money related arrangement and monetary dependability.

ATMs:

ATMs are far reaching in Estonia and can be tracked down in many towns and urban communities. They acknowledge most significant credit and check cards, including Visa and Mastercard. ATMs are accessible 24 hours per day, and a few banks offer portable applications that permit clients to pull out cash without a card.

Trade rates:
The Euro is a generally exchanged cash, and its swapping scale can fluctuate contingent upon different financial and political variables. The conversion standard between the Euro and different currencies is not set in stone by the unfamiliar trade market. Unfamiliar trade workplaces and banks in Estonia offer money trade administrations for the two occupants and travelers.

Safety And Security

Estonia has gained critical headway in guaranteeing the wellbeing and security of its residents and guests, both in the physical and computerized areas. The nation's exceptional police force, high level crisis reaction framework, and secure web-based foundation make it a protected and alluring objective for sightseers and financial backers. Estonia's obligation to network protection likewise deserves it a standing as a forerunner in computerized development and security.

Lately, Estonia has likewise earned respect for major areas of strength for its to somewhere safe and security, both in the physical and computerized spaces. In this thorough substance, we will investigate the different measures taken by Estonia to guarantee the security and security of its residents and guests.

Actual Wellbeing and Security:

Estonia is viewed as perhaps the most secure country on the planet. The crime percentage is somewhat low, and the police force is exceptional to manage any episodes that might happen. The Estonian Police and Boundary Gatekeeper Board (PPA) is liable for keeping up with the rule of law in the country. The PPA works under the purview of the Service of the Inside and has a few divisions, including the Boundary Gatekeeper, Criminal Police, and Public Request Police.

The Line Watchman division is answerable for controlling Estonia's boundaries and forestalling unlawful movement and carrying. The division utilizes cutting edge innovation, like robots and warm imaging cameras, to screen the boundary regions. The Lawbreaker Police division examines and settles violations, including robbery, extortion, and cybercrime. The Public Request Police division keeps public control and gives security to public occasions.

Estonia has an advanced crisis reaction framework that incorporates police, fire, and emergency vehicle administrations. In the event of a crisis, residents can dial 112, a widespread crisis number that associates them to the fitting help.

Estonia is likewise one of a handful of the nations on the planet to have executed a public arrangement of computerized character. This framework, known as e-Residency, permits non-occupants to lay out a computerized personality in Estonia and access different web-based administrations. The framework is secure and has a few layers of validation, making it hard for programmers to acquire unapproved access.

Computerized Wellbeing and Security:

Estonia is viewed as a world forerunner in computerized innovation, and this has prompted the nation confronting remarkable difficulties in the computerized space. Estonia has gone to a few lengths to guarantee the wellbeing and security of its computerized framework.

The nation has executed a solid web based casting a ballot framework, which has been utilized in a few public and nearby races. The framework utilizes advanced encryption and verification strategies to guarantee the trustworthiness of the democratic interaction.

Estonia has likewise settled a public network safety methodology that expects to shield its computerized framework from digital dangers. The methodology incorporates measures like ordinary security appraisals, digital occurrence reaction plans, and mindfulness raising lobbies for residents and organizations.

The public authority of Estonia has likewise settled a few establishments to regulate network protection. The Estonian Data Framework Authority (RIA) is answerable for the security and trustworthiness of Estonia's data frameworks, while the Estonian Digital protection Committee gives key direction on network safety issues.

The most effective method to be Safe in Estonia

Estonia is by and large a safe nation, however it means quite a bit to play it safe to guarantee your wellbeing and security.

By monitoring your environmental elements, protecting your resources, utilizing sound judgment while utilizing public transportation and ATMs, regarding neighborhood regulations and customs, keeping up- to-date on recent developments, and knowing how to contact crisis administrations, you can partake in a protected and pleasant excursion to Estonia.

Know about your environmental factors
Perhaps the main thing you can do to remain protected in Estonia is to know about your environmental factors.

Focus on what's going on around you, and remain alert in places, for example, train stations, transport stops, and vacation spots.

Try not to walk alone around evening time, and assuming that you should do as such, stick to sufficiently bright and populated regions.

Protect your resources

Estonia is by and large a protected nation, however like whatever other spot, there are pickpockets and cheats searching for obvious objectives. To guard your resources, keep your wallet, telephone, and other significant things in a protected area, for example, a zippered pocket or a cross-body sack. Try not to leave your sacks or different things unattended, particularly out in the open spots.

Utilize good judgment while utilizing public transportation

Estonia has a broad public transportation framework, including transports, cable cars, and trains. While these methods of transport are by and large protected, it's essential to utilize good judgment while utilizing them.

Watch out for your things, particularly while utilizing swarmed public transportation. Attempt to try not to utilize public transportation late around evening time, and assuming that you should, stick to sufficiently bright and populated courses.

Be wary while utilizing ATMs

While involving ATMs in Estonia, be wary and mindful of your environmental elements. Attempt to utilize ATMs situated inside banks or other secure areas, and try not to utilize machines that seem harmed or altered. Cover the keypad while entering your PIN, and be ready for anybody who seems, by all accounts, to be watching you.

Regard neighborhood regulations and customs

To remain protected in Estonia, regarding neighborhood regulations and customs is significant. Make a point to get to know nearby regulations and guidelines, and try not to take part in any unlawful or problematic exercises. Also, be aware of neighborhood customs and customs, like clothing regulations and strict practices.

Keep awake to-date on recent developments

It's dependably smart to keep up- to-date on recent developments in Estonia. Check neighborhood news hotspots for data on any potential well being concerns or security dangers, and know about any tourism warnings given by your nation of origin's international safe haven or department.

Know how to contact crisis administrations

If there should be an occurrence of a crisis, it means quite a bit to know how to contact crisis administrations in Estonia. The crisis telephone number in Estonia is 112, which can be utilized to contact the police, local group of fire-fighters, and emergency vehicle administrations. Try to save this number in your telephone and ability to utilize it.

Language and communication

Estonian, often known as keel, is the official tongue of Estonia, a northern European country. It is a Uralic language that is part of the Finno-Ugric language family, together with Finnish, Hungarian, and numerous other languages spoken primarily in northern Europe.

History:

Estonian has a long and complicated history. Its roots can be traced back to the proto-Finnic language used by the Finno-Ugric peoples who migrated from Siberia to northeastern Europe around 4,000 years ago. The present Estonian language began to emerge in the 13th century, when Estonia was first invaded by Holy Roman Empire Germanic-speaking crusaders. Estonian has been extensively impacted by German, Russian, and Swedish, as well as other Baltic and Slavic languages, over the years.

Grammar:

Estonian is an agglutinative language, which means it extensively relies on affixes to express tense, case, mood, and other grammatical aspects. For example, the verb "sööma" (to eat) can be inflected into a number of various forms, including "söön" (I eat), "sööd" (you eat), "sööb" (he/she/it eats), "sööme" (we eat), "sööte" (you all eat), and "söövad" (they eat).

Estonian has a number of regional dialects, each with its own pronunciation, grammar, and vocabulary. The northern dialects, spoken in Tallinn and the surrounding area, and the southern dialects, spoken in Tartu and the southern half of the country, are the two primary dialect groupings.

Usage:

Estonian is the official language of Estonia, and the vast majority of the population speaks it. Several neighboring countries, including Finland, Russia, and Latvia, recognize it as a minority language.

Communication:

Estonian is the official language, and it is widely spoken throughout the country. Due to the country's complicated past, however, many Estonians are also fluent in Russian and German. Many young people speak English, and it is becoming more popular among the younger population.

In Estonia, there are numerous ways to communicate, including:

Mobile Phones: Mobile phones are widely used in Estonia, and nearly everyone has one. Telia, Elisa, and Tele2 are among the mobile service providers in Estonia.

Internet: Estonia is noted for its excellent digital infrastructure, and it boasts one of the world's highest rates of internet usage. The internet is extensively available throughout the country, and the majority of people have high-speed broadband connection.

While the use of landline phones has declined in recent years, they are still available in many Estonian homes and businesses.

Postal Service: The Estonian Postal Service, known as Omniva, delivers mail and packages across the country. Omniva also provides a number of digital services, such as e-invoicing and e-archiving.

Email: is a popular form of communication in Estonia, and most people have email accounts through their businesses or internet service providers.

Social Media: Estonia, like many other nations, has a strong social media presence, with popular platforms such as Facebook, Instagram, and Twitter among its population.

Instant Messaging: Apps like WhatsApp, Viber, and Telegram are popular for personal and professional communication in Estonia.

Greetings

Tere! That translates to "Hello!" in Estonian.

Other common Estonian greetings are:

Tervist! "Greetings!" says the speaker.
Homikust, Tere! "Good morning!" says the speaker.
Thank you very much! "Good day!"
Greetings, Tere htust! "Good evening!" says the speaker.
Nägemist! - "Goodbye!"

Tips For Travelers

If you are planning a trip to Estonia, here are some tips to help you make the most of your visit:

Plan your trip in advance: Estonia has a lot to offer, and planning your trip in advance will help you make the most of your time. Consider the time of year you plan to visit, the places you want to see, and the activities you want to do.

Pack appropriately: Estonia has a temperate climate, and the weather can be unpredictable. It's best to pack clothes that can be layered, including a waterproof jacket, warm socks, and comfortable shoes for walking.

Learn some basic Estonian: Although many Estonians speak English, it's always a good idea to learn a few basic phrases in Estonian. This will show that you are making an effort to connect with the local culture and will help you navigate the country more easily.

Use public transportation: Estonia has a reliable and efficient public transportation system that includes buses, trams, and trains. It's a great way to explore the country and save money on transportation costs.

Try the local cuisine: Estonian cuisine is a unique blend of traditional Nordic and Baltic flavors. Be sure to try some of the local specialties, such as black bread, smoked fish, and sauerkraut.

Visit the Old Towns: Estonia is home to several well-preserved medieval Old Towns, including Tallinn, Tartu, and Viljandi. These charming towns are filled with historic buildings, quaint cobblestone streets, and picturesque squares.

Experience the outdoors: Estonia is known for its beautiful countryside, national parks, and coastline. Take the opportunity to explore the great outdoors, whether it's hiking in the forest, cycling along the coast, or swimming in one of the many lakes.

Visit during a festival: Estonia is known for its lively festivals and events, such as the Tallinn Christmas Market, the Viljandi Folk Festival, and the Song Festival. Attending one of these festivals is a great way to experience Estonian culture and traditions.

Be respectful of local customs: Estonians are friendly and welcoming, but it's important to be respectful of their customs and traditions. For example, it's customary to remove your shoes when entering someone's home, and it's considered impolite to raise your voice or speak loudly in public.

Enjoy the sauna: Saunas are a big part of Estonian culture, and there are many public saunas throughout the country. It's a great way to relax and unwind after a long day of sightseeing, and it's also a great way to connect with locals.

Conclusion

Estonia is a lovely and intriguing country with a unique combination of natural beauty, ancient history, and modern culture. Estonia has something for every sort of traveler, from the ancient Old Town of Tallinn to the picturesque forests and islands of the countryside.

Tallinn's well-preserved architecture and history are among the attractions of Estonia. The historic walls, turrets, and cobblestone streets of the city transport visitors back to the Middle Ages. Estonia also boasts a rich cultural past, with traditional music and dancing remaining an important part of daily life.

With over 2,000 islands and a broad range of landscapes, including woods, lakes, and marshes, the country is also noted for its natural beauty. This makes Estonia a perfect location for outdoor enthusiasts, with hiking, cycling, kayaking, and other activities available.

Estonia is also a digital innovation pioneer, with a strong high-tech infrastructure and a bustling startup culture. As a result, it is an excellent choice for digital nomads, entrepreneurs, and anybody interested in technology and innovation.

In practical terms, Estonia is a safe and economical destination with strong transportation links, including a well-connected public transportation system and a dependable road network. The country is also noted for having a high level of living, as well as having great healthcare and education systems.

Overall, Estonia is a must-see for anyone with an interest in history, culture, nature, or technology. Estonia has something for everyone, whether you seek a relaxing vacation or an exciting adventure.